Genesis to Revelation:

A Collection of Bible Poems

by

Helene Moolman

Genesis to Revelation: A Collection of Bible Poems

No part of this book may be reproduced or transmitted in any form or by any means, graphic, electronic, or mechanical, including photocopying, recording, taping or by any information storage or retrieval system, without the permission in writing from the publisher.

ISBN: 978-0-578-70778-5

Printed in the United States of America

Dedication

To my four daughters: Helene, Elna, Linda and Annette.
You bring so much joy into my life.

Table of Contents

The Old Testament

CREATION

God looked down on planet Earth, so barren, dark and cold,
In Genesis the wonders of creation's story is told.
God's almighty Spirit over moving water stood,
His master plan for all mankind that He designed was good.
"Let there be light," God said aloud and shining light was born;
Light was day and darkness night – the world's very first morn.

On the second day God made the sky by separating waters,
The ones below and those above were sent to their very own quarters.
And God was pleased when His creation listened,
And He saw how the light on the waters glistened.
Then God caused the waters to recede to a special place,
The ocean now had boundaries set by the Creator's pace.
Dry ground appeared which He called land,
And the waves rolled gently over the sand.

On day number three God looked all around,
Nothing grew above or under the ground.
Suddenly His voice was heard calling once again,
Earth would now produce green plants, fruit trees and grain.
On day number four God made two powerful lights,
The moon by night – the sun by day – what wonderful sights!
The stars began to twinkle and God said: "It is good!"
His eyes were alight with pleasure as on planet Earth He stood.

On day number five He created life in the ocean and in the sky.
"Let there be birds," He said and gave them strong wings to fly.
Then He filled the turbulent sea with fishes big and small,
And wondrous living creatures on the seabed did crawl.
God spoke again to planet Earth and animals appeared,
Some were tame and others wild and reptiles' heads were reared.

Genesis to Revelation

The Lord our God, the Three in One, the sixth day fashioned man.
He breathed the breath of life in humans according to His plan.
He called them Man and Woman and blessed them mightily.
"Fill the earth with people – enjoy what I've created so abundantly!"

But when day seven came along, the Lord our God did rest.
And when He looked at planet Earth, He knew He'd done His best.
Everything was perfect and the Creator could rejoice,
When He'd spoken the words of life, creation had heeded His voice!

NOAH – TO BUILD AN ARK

To build an ark
Is not a stroll in the park!
When the soil is just like dust
And only God you can trust,
When the sun is beating down
And people pass you with a frown,
It takes an upright man
To carry out God's plan.

To build an ark
Is not a stroll in the park!
When while the ship takes shape,
People stare and sneer and gape,
You gaze up at the sky
But never say: "God, why?"
It takes a man with grit
To say: "I will not quit!"

To build an ark
Is not a stroll in the park!
When animals great and small
Come at Noah's urgent call
And they go in two by two,
Though there's no sign of rain or dew,
It takes a humble man
To say: "Lord, here I am."

To build an ark
Is not a stroll in the park!
When God sends out the crow
It's just to let you know
His love surrounds us all.
And when we hear His call
In thankfulness we'll say:
"We love You more each day."

JOSEPH

Joseph was Jacob and Rachel's son,
Of all his brothers, he was the favorite one.
His many colored coat was a gift from his dad,
His reports about his brothers made them hopping mad.

When Joseph started dreaming of sheaves of grain and stars in the sky,
Telling them they'd be bowing before him before they die,
His brothers hated him more each day,
Even his father's heart was filled with dismay!

Joseph's brothers grazed their flocks
in the fields one day;
Jacob sent Joseph to see how they were doing
and he went on his way.
But when his brothers saw him
they hatched an evil plot,
"Let's kill him," they all shouted,
"and rid us of this blot!
We'll dip his coat in an animal's blood
and tell our father he's dead,"
But Ruben rescued Joseph
and threw him in a pit instead.

While the brothers were sitting down to eat,
they saw Ishmaelites coming their way.
They sold their brother to those people as a slave,
for in the pit he could not stay.
When Jacob heard that Joseph was dead,
he bowed his head and wept.
His sons tried to comfort their old father,
but nothing had any effect.

An Egyptian captain named Potiphar
bought Joseph and took him home.
But the captain's wife looked at Joseph
and her eyes began to roam!
Potiphar chose to believe
the lies of his deceitful wife,
And soon Joseph was thrown into prison –
a place of violence and strife.

But God Almighty saw all that had happened
and was with Joseph each day.
"Listen to Joseph," the warden said –
"his orders you must obey!"
Two men in Joseph's custody
both had a dream one night,
And soon after,
Joseph saw a change in his terrible plight.

"Tell me your dreams and do not fear,"
Joseph told the two troubled men,
"for Almighty God will tell me all
and His word is yea and amen."
Pharaoh's butler received good news –
as cup bearer he would be restored;
The baker however would not be forgiven –
for him there would be no reward.

Two years later Pharaoh's dreams troubled him
as he lay on his bed at night,
And although he thought about what they meant,
he just could not get it right.
Seven cows stood beside the Nile –
they were healthy and fat and round,
But soon seven skinny cows came along
and devoured them pound by pound.
The skinny cows stayed just as thin
after enjoying their great big meal.

"These dreams mean something," Pharaoh said.
"To my wise men I will appeal!"

"Take note, oh Pharaoh," Joseph said,
"for seven years you'll have plenty of bread;
Then there will follow seven years of famine
and people will be starving instead.
Choose a man who has understanding and is wise,
let him store up grain in the cities far and wide.
When the famine sweeps over the land,
we'll be ready and take what happens in our stride."

When Jacob heard that there was grain in Egypt,
he sent his sons to buy food.
When Joseph saw his brothers, he said they were spies –
"You're up to no good."
"Bring your youngest brother to me," Joseph said,
"then I'll know your words are true."
Simeon stayed behind as ransom
and they left without further ado!

Along the way one of them, while feeding his donkey,
found his money in his sack.
"This is God's punishment," they said,
"for what we did to Joseph so many years back."
After telling their father everything,
he relented and let Benjamin go,
If he lost his youngest son as well,
it would be the final blow.

On their journey home, Joseph's silver cup
in Benjamin's sack was found.
With fear and trembling they went back to Egypt –
before Joseph they bowed to the ground.
But Joseph, weeping, told his brothers who he was
and forgave them their deeds of the past.

"Bring my old father to me in Egypt –
we'll be united as a family at last."

Jacob and his sons lived in the land of Goshen,
tending their flocks of sheep.
Joseph looked after his family,
for Pharaoh had given them into his keep.
Two sons were born to Joseph
and he became a hundred and ten years old,
And so the wonderful story of Joseph
for years to come will be told.

THE TEN PLAGUES

Pharaoh lived in Egypt – he was a mighty king!
But God saw from heaven just what was happening.
His chosen race, the Israelites, were made to work as slaves,
Many died in poverty – were laid to rest in graves.

Moses and his brother, Aaron, listened to God's voice;
He sent them down to Egypt – not giving them a choice.
"Tell the king of Egypt to let my people go.
If he does not listen, My wrath will not be slow!"

Pharaoh treated Moses with pride and with disdain.
"These slaves are all just lazy, so I'll increase their daily pain.
No more straw they'll get from me to make their piles of bricks,
And if they don't complete their tasks, I'll break their backs with sticks!"

God sent Moses and his brother to the swiftly flowing Nile.
Moses struck the water which soon bled blood – so vile!
But Pharaoh's magic makers laughed and did the same.
"We are just as mighty as your God," they loudly did proclaim.

The second plague we read about had all to do with frogs.
They jumped around in pots and pans, in beds and in the bogs.
But Moses asked Almighty God to take the plague away.
And even then the king said: "NO! The slaves just had to stay!"

"Strike the ground now, Moses! I'll punish them with gnats;
They'll bite the people all day long – even under their hats."
But Pharaoh had a stubborn heart and when the gnats had gone,
He would not let the people go – he thought that he had won.

The next two plagues that God did send
were flies and deadly disease.
The awful flies swarmed everywhere

and made the people sneeze!
The horses, camels, sheep and goats
were ill and lay in heaps,
But Pharaoh said the slaves would stay:
"They're mine," he said, "for keeps!"

"Now," God ordered, "take ashes from the stove
and throw it in the air;
I'll inflict everyone with sores,
more than they can bear!"
They itched and scratched and groaned and moaned –
their bodies were on fire
And Pharaoh's disobedience
brought down God's wrath and ire!

The next two plagues were locusts
and hailstones raining down.
The hailstones stripped the bark from trees
in every village and town.
The locusts ate the crops
till nothing green remained,
But Pharaoh chased the brothers away –
they were up to no good, he claimed.

"Stretch your arm toward the sky,"
the Lord to Moses said.
"I'll cover the land in darkness
and fill the people with dread."
And all was silent for three long days
while the people stayed at home.
Even the king and his household
did not dare to roam.

Once more Moses went to the king to tell him what God said:
At midnight everyone's firstborn would die in his bed.
Pharaoh had been told by him to let God's people go,
But after every plague had gone, the king kept saying: "No!"

**Helene Moolman

The Israelites were told to prepare a goat or a lamb.
This had been decreed by God – the great I Am!
The blood of the animals was sprinkled around the doors,
They had to do it quickly – not even stop or pause!

At daybreak on the following day the firstborn all were dead.
The people mourned and cried aloud as news of the disaster spread.
Pharaoh, who had lost a son, at last obeyed God's voice.
The Israelites prepared a feast and started to rejoice!

Thank you, my Lord Almighty God, that You set the captives free.
Thank you Lord, that You sent Your Son to save a sinner like me.
And as the Israelites prepared a feast to honor You that day,
Be our Guide and lead us, Lord – come in our hearts to stay.

SAMSON

Samson was a Nazirite,
Against the Philistines he would fight.
A pair of scissors was never to come near his hair;
Alas he loved women ever so fair!

He killed a fierce lion with his huge strong hands;
He let burning foxes loose in the enemy's lands.
He killed a thousand men with the jawbone of a mule,
He ripped out a city's gates – challenged the enemy to a duel.

Delilah lived in a Philistine city.
Samson thought she loved him – oh, what a pity!
She kept on asking him about his strength;
He grew so frustrated that he gave in at length.

"Bind me with bowstrings, and then I'll be weak;
or tie me up with ropes if my death you do seek.
Perhaps if you weave my seven locks in a loom,
You can catch me and carry me out of this room."

But no matter how hard the Philistines tried,
Samson broke the fetters with which he was tied.

Then one day Samson could take it no more.
"Cut off my hair, Delilah, then I'll have no strength left in store!"
And that's what she did as Samson lay sleeping;
He was caught and given into his enemies' keeping.

Samson was blinded and treated as a slave,

He was forced to grind flour at the mill like a knave.
But what the Philistines did not know,
Was that Samson's hair had started to grow.

The Philistines held a feast one day.
"Call Samson," they said, "and we'll watch him play!"
The house where they feasted stood high above the ground;
Samson wrapped his arms round two pillars he had found.

"Oh Lord my God, hear my prayers, hear my sighs,
Avenge this day my two blind eyes."
Samson bowed forward, crushed the pillars in two,
More than three thousand people that day he slew.

Samson's family came that day
and buried him near his father's grave.
There is only one God who rules this world,
only He is able to save!

GIDEON

The people of Midian said to each other:
"The crops of the Jews we'll destroy,
Soon they'll have nothing more to eat,
no more peace they will enjoy!"
They came in their thousands
with their camels and their cattle.
"We'll conquer these Jews,
we are ready for battle!"

Gideon was beating wheat one day
when he saw an angel beneath a big oak tree.
"God wants to use you," the angel said.
"You are upright, fearless and brave.
Your God will be with you every day
as your people you will save."

Gideon spoke to God and asked Him for a sign
to make sure what he'd heard was true.
He placed a fleece of wool on the ground
and asked God to cover it with dew.
"Let the fleece be wet, but the ground be dry,
then I'll know the message is from You."

God in His mercy answered Gideon's plea,
but he still asked God for more.
"Please God," Gideon said, "let the fleece be dry
and the ground be wet,
then I'll believe Your message
and no more I'll fret."

God answered Gideon's every plea
and all his demands He met.

Gideon gathered his army together,
in the valley of Morek was their camp.
"Your army is too big," God said.
"On only three hundred men I'll place my stamp.
It is I who will win this battle for you;
the people will see my Glory.
For generations to come nations will rejoice
when they read this wonderful story."

Every soldier was given a trumpet
and an empty pitcher with a torch inside.
"Do just as I do," Gideon told his men.
"We'll do just as you say!" they cried.
They blew their trumpets and broke their pitchers.
"For the Lord and Gideon!" they roared.
In their left hands they held their torches
and they never even needed a sword.

The Midianites heard the noise in the night;
they jumped right out of their beds.
They ran around dazed and confused,
pointing their swords at each other's heads!
Gideon and his loyal men,
with God's help, restored the land.
The people were able to plant new crops
that would soon grow in the sand.

RUTH

Elimelech and his wife Naomi lived in Bethlehem
Their sons Mahlon and Chilion also stayed with them.
But soon there came a hot and very dusty drought
And the family left and said, "We must get out!"

They slowly made their way to Moab
where they agreed to stay;
But soon Naomi's husband died
and her sons married without delay!
The one took Orpah
and the other took Ruth,
But all too soon they also died
and left their mom to face the truth.

"I'll go back to my country," she said with a sigh.
"The drought is over and there's food I can buy."
Her daughters-in-law said, "We will stay at your side."
But Orpah changed her mind while many tears she cried.

"I'll not leave you or forsake you,"
Ruth then said aloud.
"Your God will also be my God,"
to her mother-in-law she vowed.
They traveled on for many days
until they came back home
And Ruth stayed there in Bethlehem
never more to roam.

Now Boaz was a wealthy man
who had a great big farm.
He was a good and gentle man
and the reapers knew no harm.
When Ruth went out to gather grain,
he saw her and took pity.
"Leave her alone," he told the men,
"for she's new here in the city."

Naomi said to Boaz her cousin,
"Come buy my field and all that is mine.
Ruth will then become your wife
and that would suit you just fine!"
Ruth and Boaz had a baby boy
and Obed was his name;
And all her friends rejoiced with Naomi
for God had taken away her pain.

DAVID AND GOLIATH

King Saul and his army were preparing for a fight,
Their enemies, the Philistines were an awesome sight!
On a hill, one morning, there stood a gigantic man,
His name was Goliath and from him the Israelites ran!

"Choose a man to fight me!" he bellowed night and day,
"I'm big and strong and fearless – I'll beat him come what may!"
When Saul and all the Israelites heard what Goliath said,
They all began to tremble – the camp was filled with dread.

David was a shepherd boy
who looked after his father's sheep,
He stayed alert while watching them,
for the flocks were in his keep.
His father sent him with food to his brothers –
he was eager to hear some news,
But his brothers were angry when they heard him ask
about the giant fighting the Jews!

"I will fight this heathen man," David said to Saul,
But when he put on his armor, all he did was fall!
"My God Who delivered me from the lion and the bear,
Will help me fight this battle, my life is in His care."

Five smooth, round stones David took and put one in his sling.
Quickly he walked to face the giant, not fearing anything.
"I'll give your flesh to the birds and the beasts," a cursing Goliath said.
"If you come any nearer, I'll strike you down and soon you will be dead!"

Then David shouted:
"I come to you in the Name of my God who you chose to defy.
This day my Lord will deliver me – I'll smite you and you will die!"

Genesis to Revelation

David twirled his sling in the air and swiftly flew the stone,
It hit Goliath in the head and he fell down with a groan.

David ran to the fallen giant and killed him with his sword.
The Israelites rushed out of the camp. "We won the battle!" they roared.
David trusted Almighty God for the rest of his days,
And when he wrote the beautiful psalms, he always gave God praise.

ELIJAH AND THE PROPHETS OF BAAL

King Ahab ruled over Israel –
he was disobedient to God's commands.
His wife's name was Jezebel –
he was like putty in her hands.
She was a wicked queen
and led the people astray;
She called them all together and said:
"It's to Baal that you must pray!"

Now God called the prophet Elijah
and made known to him His plan.
"Tell Ahab to summon the people,
every child, woman and man.
Send for the prophets of Baal,
I want them all to be there.
I'll teach these people a lesson,
My glory I will not share."

Elijah quickly took two bulls
and cut them into pieces.
The one bull he laid on the altar to Baal,
together with their meat and their fleeces.
"Now place the meat on the wood," he said,
"but do not yet set it alight.
Call to your god to send fire from heaven,
let's see his strength and his might!"

The prophets of Baal called aloud to their god
from early morning till noon.
"Call louder!" Elijah taunted them.
"Perhaps he'll hear you real soon!"
But no one answered the shouting prophets –
their god made of stone was dead.
"Come near me," Elijah said to the people
and swiftly walked ahead.

The altar of God was quickly rebuilt –
Elijah used twelve big stones.
The prophets of Baal had cut themselves –
the people heard their groans.
A trench was made around the altar
and the meat was placed on top.
"Pour water over everything –
keep on pouring till I say: "Stop!"

Then Elijah called on the Name of the Lord,
the Mighty One on the throne.
"Lord, send fire from heaven," he prayed,
"for I know You are God alone."
And as the people watched in awe,
the fire from heaven was sent –
It consumed the meat, the wood and the dust,
even the water in the trench was spent.

"The Lord is God! Yes, He is God!"
said the people of Israel.
They seized the prophets as they fled –

they were killed and lay where they fell.
God in His mercy sent rain that day,
the wind-swept clouds were black.
The miracle God performed that day
brought His people back on track!

NEHEMIAH

Nehemiah was the son of old Hacaliah.
I don't think he was related to the prophet Isaiah!
But while he was in Persia, his brother brought the news,
"Jerusalem's walls are broken – come save your fellow Jews!"

Nehemiah sadly bent his head and went down on his knees,
To Almighty God in heaven he raised his heartfelt pleas.
"I'm needed by my people in Jerusalem, Lord,
The walls around the city must be restored!"

When the king heard why Nehemiah was so sad,
By God's mercy and grace, he wasn't even mad.
He gave Nehemiah letters to safeguard them all,
And he and his men rushed off to answer God's call.

When Nehemiah arrived in the darkened city,
He looked around him with a heart filled with pity.
But as the people gathered their much needed tools,
Sanballat and Tobiah arrived with their book of rules.

The people were excited – each family built a section
And strapped to their bodies they had swords for protection.
Sanballat and Tobiah were laughing them to scorn,
But the Jews kept building till every beam was sawn.

Sanballat and Tobiah ranted and raved,
But from the evil plot Nehemiah was saved.
And when the walls were done, the people stood in awe,
As Esra came before them, reading from God's Law.

Nehemiah told the people:
"Come celebrate this special day
with wine and wholesome food,
The walls have been completed –
our God is good!"
And then he interceded
for his people on his knees:
"Forgive us all our sins oh Lord –
it's You we want to please."

When things around us start to crumble
and our walls begin to crack,
Let's put on God's whole armor –
never looking back.
Like soldiers let's do battle
and win the victory,
And celebrate anew each day
God's love for you and me.

DANIEL

Darius lived in Babylon
and there he reigned as king.
"You're an upright man," he told Daniel
and made him ruler of everything.
There were men, however, who hated Daniel –
they were cruel, jealous and mean,
So they plotted to have Daniel killed
and they made their plans unseen.

"Darius, oh king," they said to him,
"we want you to make a decree,
Anyone who bows to any god
but you must be killed, don't you agree?"
But Daniel loved the Lord his God
and prayed to Him three times a day.
He was obedient to the One who protected him,
whatever came his way.

When the wicked men saw Daniel praying,
they stormed the king's throne with glee.
"Throw him in the lions' den," they shouted.
"And don't try to set him free!"
Hearing these words the king was distressed
and tried to stop the men,
But because he'd made a solemn decree,
they threw Daniel in the lions' den.

King Darius went back to this palace –
all night he never slept.

As soon as the sun began to shine,
out of his bed he leapt!
He ran to the lions' den in haste crying,
"Daniel, did your god keep you safe through the night?"
Daniel answered that his God had sent an angel
who'd shut the lions' mouths real tight!

The king rejoiced and was very glad
when Daniel was rescued from the lions' den.
"Who did this to Daniel?" said the king –
"Bring to me those wicked men!
Throw them to the hungry lions instead –
with their lives they all will pay!"
Then all the people praised Daniel's God
and prayed to Him each day.

JONAH

God spoke to Jonah one day long ago:
"Go to the city Nineveh and let the people know:
Your sins have come before Me, says the Lord most High,
and if you do not soon repent, all of you must die!"

But Jonah fled to Joppa and there he found a ship
And soon he and the sailors set out on a perilous trip.
God, however, sent a mighty wind that tossed the waves up high;
The frightened men on board the ship let out a fearful cry!

The captain called to Jonah who quietly lay sleeping:
"Ask your God to rescue us," he cried out almost weeping.
When the crew had cast the lot to find the guilty one,
Jonah was the culprit – from Almighty God you do not run!

Then Jonah said: "Take me up and throw me into the sea,
and soon enough from the tempest you'll be free."
After the storm had ceased to rage, the crew went on their knees
and thanked the Lord for mercifully answering their pleas.

As Jonah hit the water, God sent a great big fish;
It opened its mouth and gleefully swallowed the tasty dish!
Jonah now found himself in the monster fish's belly
And suddenly he trembled and his bones turned to jelly!

Three days and three nights Jonah rolled around –
tossed to and fro,
It was dark inside and he was covered
in seaweed from head to toe.
But when God told him once again
to listen when He spoke,
Jonah said: "Yes Lord, I'll go –
lying in the fish's tummy was certainly no joke!"

Genesis to Revelation

Men and women heard Jonah preach, even the king upon his throne:
"Forty days are all that's left before by God you'll be overthrown!"
The king then made a solemn decree while sitting in sackcloth and ashes:
"No one will drink or eat anything – neither meat nor potato hashes!
Let everyone turn from their evil ways – from the violence in their hands.
Cry out to God in mercy, to the One who understands."

God saw their works when they turned from their evil ways;
He forgave them and restored them after forty long days.
But Jonah was angry and asked God to take his life;
Then he would be free from all evil and all strife.
While Jonah watched the city, God made a plant to grow.
It sheltered Jonah from the sun, from every red hot glow.
But soon a worm destroyed the plant and Jonah felt the heat;
The sultry east wind nearly blew him off his feet.

Jonah heard God speak to him
of His infinite love and grace
And when we repent of all our sins,
Our God has a smile on His face.

ESTHER

Ahasuerus was a Persian king, a mighty ruler was he.
He invited his people to his palace: "Come enjoy a feast with me!"
He showed them many beautiful things;
His hangings of linen had silver rings.
His couches were made of solid gold.
"Enjoy all the food," the people were told.

Queen Vashti lived in the royal house.
When invited to the feast, she disobeyed her spouse.
The king was angry and asked for advice:
The queen had to go – she would pay the price.
The king was sad for he longed for a bride;
For a queen he could love, who would sit at his side.

Pretty young women came to the palace each day –
Some were not suitable – others were asked to stay.
Esther, a Jewish woman, was one of those who stayed.
Her uncle, Mordecai loved her – for her he daily prayed.
Haman, an important official, was angered by Mordecai.
He never bowed to Haman as he proudly strutted by.

For twelve long months Esther was bathed
in oils and spices sweet.
Early one day she was taken away
for she and the king would meet.
The king chose Esther to be his bride
and placed a crown on her head.
"Let's all rejoice and have a feast,"
King Ahasuerus said,

But Haman was hatching an evil plot
to wipe out all the Jews
And soon Mordecai sent for Esther
to tell her all the news.

Haman's decree to kill the Jews
was signed by the king with his ring.
Mordecai told Esther to go to the king
and tell him everything.

Esther humbled herself before the king
and invited him to dinner.
When Haman heard he'd also be going
there was no stopping that old sinner!
He told his wife and sons at home:
"I'm very important, you know!
I'll make a gallows and hang Mordecai –
his death will not be slow!"

One night the book of memorable deeds
was read to the restless king.
"I see that the Jew, Mordecai, saved my life
when death was a certain thing.
Dress this man in my royal robes,
put my crown upon his head.
Say the king wants to honor him
as through the square he's led."
Haman was told to lead the procession
and horrified he obeyed,
And when he told his wife what had happened,
he trembled and was afraid.

The king and Haman came to Esther
and sat at the table to eat.
"Please listen to me, my king,"
Esther said as she got up from her seat.
"This evil man, Haman, has plotted
and planned to have my people killed."
"Have mercy on me!" evil Haman pleaded
as words from his mouth were spilled.
"Take him away!" king Ahasuerus said.
"He'll hang for what he's done!"
The Jews rejoiced when they heard the news –
they praised God, yes, everyone.

EZEKIEL – DRY BONES

Ezekiel was a prophet chosen by the Lord –
The words from his mouth were like a two-edged sword.
God sent him down the road to a valley one day,
And what he saw before him filled his heart with dismay.

On the dusty ground he saw thousands of bones,
They were scattered all over the sand and the stones.
The scene of desolation and the silence all around,
stirred him so profoundly that he fell to the ground.

Suddenly God spoke to him and calmed his every fear;
Everything was possible when the great I Am was near.
"Tell these bones, Ezekiel, to listen when I speak,
I want to bring them back to life, give strength to the weak."

Ezekiel shouted to the wind: "The Lord commands you: 'Blow!'
Direct your breath towards these bones, don't miss a single row!"
And soon there came a rattling noise and limbs began to stir,
But God did not once mistake a him for a her!

The first to move were all the heads and much to their surprise,
Because they had no necks attached, none of them could rise!
But soon the wind blew once again and God provided necks
And soon the bones were covered with super special pecs!

Their arms and legs were soon attached and muscles began to show
And God in His mercy made their nails and hair to grow.
Soon the mighty army stood firmly on their feet,
Ezekiel praised Almighty God that his mission was complete.

God's promise to His people
was that He'd open up their graves,
He'd set them free and let them live
because He's the one who saves.
His Spirit is the breath of life –
an ever burning flame,
And if you give your life to Him,
you'll never be the same.

The New Testament

JESUS OUR REDEEMER

God said to His precious Son one day:
"To planet Earth I'm sending you away.
The people made in our image have sinned;
they've sadly all gone astray."
In Bethlehem Jesus was born
in a stable while angels sang about peace,
And thirty three years later
our Savior paid the price for our release.

Many miracles Jesus performed on earth –
He changed water into wine,
He healed the lepers, made the blind to see
and the deaf could hear just fine.
He raised Jairus' daughter from the dead,
from devils He set people free,
He spoke to the people, told them to repent
although the Pharisees did not always agree.

He walked the dusty streets all day –
many nights He spent alone,
He prayed to His Father in heaven for strength,
to the One who sat on the throne.
He fed a multitude
with five loaves and two fishes,
The leftovers were gathered
and put into dishes.
He walked on water
and calmed a raging sea,

He raised a young man from the dead
when He heard his mother's plea.

His disciples willingly followed Him
wherever Jesus went,
When they asked Him about the parables
He told them what they meant.
He blessed all the children –
loving each smiling face,
The people thronged around Him
and marveled at His grace.
He was crucified on a cruel cross –
on the third day He rose from the dead,
When He comes back to earth
He'll judge the world – just as He said.

JESUS PAID THE PRICE

When Jesus knew His time was near
He gathered His disciples round a table and said:
"My body will be broken for all mankind,
therefore drink of this wine and eat of this bread.
One of you will betray Me this night
And after My capture you will all take flight."

Peter looked at Jesus, saying: "Lord, how can this be?
I'll stand by You through thick and thin – I'll fight to set You free!"
But three times Peter said that night: "This man I do not know!"
And then his tears ran down his face as he heard a rooster crow.

After standing trial they led Jesus away,
On His bruised and beaten body a cruel cross they lay.
And when on that cross our Savior finally died,
A cruel, sharp spear was thrust through His side.

Suddenly the sun's light faded – the temple's curtain was torn asunder!
The earth quaked and trembled – there was rolling thunder!
In the heavens above God welcomed home His only begotten Son,
He'd paid the price with His precious Blood as death He'd overcome.

Thank you Jesus that You died for me.
Thank you my Lord that from sin You set me free.
I will love and worship You with body, spirit and soul,
For You have changed my life – You have made me whole.

THE TWELVE DISCIPLES

When Jesus walked beside the sea,
He saw some fishermen from Galilee.
"Come follow Me," Jesus said aloud,
And they ran to Jesus through the crowd.

Now two of them were called Andrew and Peter,
But Andrew's brother beat him by a meter!
Peter was the one who jumped into the sea,
But when he denied his Lord he wept bitterly.
Lord, help us like Peter to jump overboard,
To be fearless and brave,
To ride the crest of a wave,
To reach out our hands so we can be restored.

James and John were the sons of Zebedee,
Called the Sons of Thunder,
They somehow made a blunder,
When they tried to secure a place,
Either side of the throne of Grace,
But Jesus heard the others grumble,
And He started to teach them to be humble.
Let us kneel at His Mercy seat,
and wash each other's feet.

The angel of the Lord said to Philip, "Go south!
An Ethiopian official needs to hear My word from your mouth.
I want you to explain about my suffering and pain,
And when from sin he's saved, in water he'll be bathed."

Genesis to Revelation

Oh Lord, help us obey all Your commands each day.

Matthew was a tax collector;
He belonged to the financial sector.
People despised him for his cunning,
But when Jesus called him, he came running!
"Sit down Lord, share my dinner.
Have compassion on me, a desperate sinner!"
Let us throw our doors open wide,
And invite the poor and needy right inside.

Now we come to doubting Thomas,
He forgot all about his Leader's promise.
"I want to see and feel," he said,
"How can I believe He was raised from the dead?"
Jesus looked at Thomas and showed him His side:
"You are my Lord and my God," Thomas cried.
Lord, help us trust in You each day,
You are the Truth, the Life, the Way!

Then there was Bartholomew, Simon and James,
The Bible does not often mention their names.
But they also listened to the Sermon on the Mount,
They saw when He healed the sick, too many to count!
And when a multitude of people had been fed,
They helped to fill the baskets with leftover bread.
Lord, You are The Lion and The Lamb,
You are our God, the Great I Am.

Judas became a traitor on that fateful night,
He kissed his faithful Master and then took flight.
And suddenly it dawned on him just what he'd done,

Helene Moolman

He'd just betrayed God's only Son, the Holy One.
"Too late, too late!" he cried aloud,
as the sun was obscured by a thick, dark cloud.
But Jesus called out, "It is done!"
The victory over death had just been won!

WHEN SAUL BECAME PAUL

When Stephen was being stoned by an angry mob,
their clothes lay at a young man's feet.
His name was Saul of Tarsis –
he approved of what was happening in the street.
He helped to persecute the Christians
and dragged them off to jail.
"I'll go to Damascus and search for those disciples,
in my mission I will not fail!"

On the road to Damascus blinding light came shining,
stopping him in his tracks.
The men who accompanied him cried in alarm
and fell in the dust on their backs.
"Why are you persecuting Me?"
a loud voice from heaven said.
"Who are You, Lord?" asked a frightened Saul
and fell to the ground in dread.

"I am Jesus," answered the voice from heaven.
"Stop persecuting Me so zealously!"
"What shall I do?" Saul asked the Lord.
"What You ask I'll do willingly."
Jesus sent Saul into the city;
for three days he could not see.
He neither ate nor drank anything;
only God could set him free.

A man called Ananias had a vision one night –
God sent him to a house in the city.

"Go to a street called Straight," He said.
"On blind Saul I will pour out my pity.
Do not be afraid of him
for my servant he will be.
He'll boldly preach the Gospel –
tell people to trust in Me."

Soon Saul became Paul and he joined the disciples,
proclaiming that Jesus was Lord.
He was beaten and stoned and put into jail
and once even fell overboard.
But he kept on telling his fellowmen
about Jesus who died on the cross.
"Come to Him all who are thirsty;
all your sins away He'll wash."

PAUL AND THE SHIPWRECK

Paul was persecuted by wicked men, who tried to have him killed.
A Roman captain rescued him as people round him milled.
"Take me to Caesar in Rome," Paul said – "to him I will appeal.
I know my God will keep me safe, my fate only He can seal."

Paul and a number of prisoners sailed on a ship around the coast.
Julius, a centurion, was kind to Paul – a very gracious host.
At a port called Fair Haven, Paul warned the captain:
"We must stop over here till spring."
"I'll not listen to you," the captain said.
"I'm in charge! I've had the proper training!"

The wind blew softly as they sailed away,
but soon came a change in the weather.
Violently they were tossed about in the sea;
they used ropes to keep the ship together.
They threw freight and furniture overboard;
they were frightened and had lost all hope.
They neither ate nor drank for many long days –
the crew could just not cope.

Paul spoke words of encouragement:
"Now everyone listen to me.
God will certainly save us all,
not one of you'll drown in the sea."
And soon the sailors were greatly cheered
as land through the mist they saw.
Although the ship broke in two on the rocks,
they all safely reached the shore.

On the island of Malta they were kindly received,
Publius was the headman's name.
When a viper bit Paul, he did not die –
to him all the sick people came.
They stayed on the island for three long months
until a ship took them all away.
And finally they safely docked in Rome
where Paul stayed till his dying day.

REVELATION

John, the beloved disciple,
was banished to Patmos near Greece.
He was told by certain people
that his preaching about Jesus must cease.
But God had a plan He wished to reveal
to a troubled, dying world.
And in visions to John miraculous happenings
were soon to be unfurled.

John saw Jesus between burning lamps,
wearing a robe and a girdle of gold.
His eyes were flashing like flames of fire,
His hair as white as snow in the cold.
His voice was like waters roaring,
His feet like burnished bronze, aglow,
From His mouth came a two-edged sword,
His face was shining like the sun we know!

And then John heard
a loud voice saying:
"I am the Alpha and the Omega,
the First and also the Last!
I am the One who died on the cross.
On the third day I rose again.
I have the keys of death in my hands.
I can heal a dying world's worst pain!"

John wrote letters to the seven churches saying:
"Be victorious and endure till the end.

Genesis to Revelation

Those who have an ear to hear,
stand fast, for the truth contend!

God will give to those who overcome,
a white stone engraved with his name.
Knock and He'll certainly open the door,
His blessings on you He'll pour."

John also saw twenty-four elders
and four living creatures standing around God's throne.
Day and night they sang their praises
to the Worthy Lamb alone.
He saw huge angels flying in heaven,
carrying the seals of God in their hands,
When they blew on their trumpets the earth was destroyed,
they carried out all God's plans.

We also read about the antichrist,
the false prophet, the dragon and the beast,
But God overcame the evil one
by the Blood of our One High Priest.
The old heaven and earth will pass away,
the new Jerusalem will be dressed like a bride,
Thousands of ten thousands will be praising God,
kneeling side by side.
You are worthy, oh Lamb of God,
Creator of everything.
You are the One Whom we adore,
as salvation's song we sing.

About the Author

Helene Moolman was born in South Africa but now lives in Kingwood, Texas with her son-in-law, Theunis and daughter, Elna. She always loved reading and writing poetry. The Bible has been her inspiration and gives her strength to face each day. May these verses bring joy to young and old.